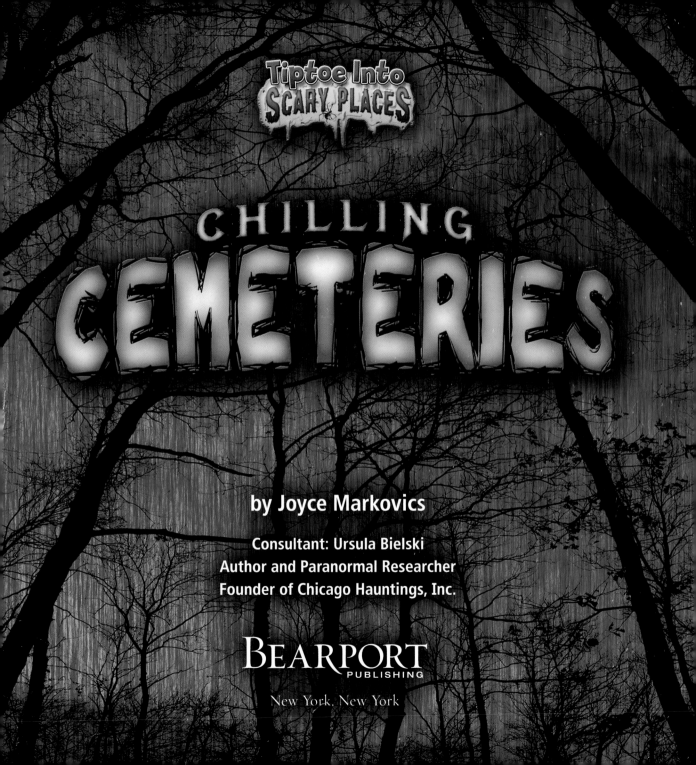

Tiptoe Into SCARY PLACES

CHILLING CEMETERIES

by Joyce Markovics

Consultant: Ursula Bielski
Author and Paranormal Researcher
Founder of Chicago Hauntings, Inc.

BEARPORT PUBLISHING

New York, New York

Credits

Cover, © khd/Shutterstock, © Fatbob/Bigstockphoto, and © Vasina Nazarenko/Fotolia; TOC, © Marcin Perkkowski/Shutterstock and © Hitdelight/Shutterstock; 4–5, © Marcin Perkowski/Shutterstock, © Hitdelight/Shutterstock, © Elena Schweitzer/Shutterstock, © Maciej Olszewski/Shutterstock, © Ryan Ladbrook/Shutterstock, © schankz/Shutterstock, © Avicha11/Shutterstock, © Vincze Szabi/Shutterstock, and © Fabien Monteil/Shutterstock; 6L, © Olinchuk/Shutterstock; 6R, © Elzbieta Sekowksa/Shutterstock; 7, © LEE SNIDER PHOTO IMAGES/Shutterstock; 8, © David Lee Tiller; 9, © David Lee Tiller; 11, © Enrique de la Cruz/supernoramx/Flickr; 12L, © serpeblu/Shutterstock; 12R, © Richard Peterson/Shutterstock; 13, © Chonlatorn/Shutterstock; 14, © Hal Hirshorn/The Merchant's House Museum/The New York City Marble Cemetery; 15, © Patrick Phillips; 16L, © Carolyn M Carpenter/Shutterstock; 16R, © Ritu Manoj Jethani/Shutterstock; 17, © Carolyn M Carpenter/Shutterstock; 18, © Mick Sinclair/Alamy; 19, © Artem Efimov/Shutterstock and © Evgeniia Litovchenko/Shutterstock; 21, © Lipowski Milan/Shutterstock, © bob8435/Shutterstock, and © Khuroshvili Ilya/Shutterstock; 23, © Ryzhkov Sergey/Shutterstock and © periscope/Shutterstock; 24, © Chokniti Khongchum/Shutterstock.

Publisher: Kenn Goin
Senior Editor: Joyce Tavolacci
Creative Director: Spencer Brinker
Photo Researcher: Thomas Persano
Cover: Kim Jones

Library of Congress Cataloging-in-Publication Data

Names: Markovics, Joyce L., author.
Title: Chilling cemeteries / by Joyce Markovics.
Description: New York, New York : Bearport Publishing, [2017] I Series:
   Tiptoe into scary places I Includes bibliographical references and index.
Identifiers: LCCN 2016037731 (print) I LCCN 2016038409 (ebook) I ISBN
   9781684020485 (library) I ISBN 9781684021000 (ebook)
Subjects: LCSH: Haunted cemeteries—Juvenile literature. I
   Cemeteries—Legends—Juvenile literature. I Haunted places—Juvenile
   literature.
Classification: LCC BF1474.3 .M37 2017 (print) I LCC BF1474.3 (ebook) I DDC
   133.1/22—dc23
LC record available at https://lccn.loc.gov/2016037731

For more information, write to Bearport Publishing Company, Inc., 45 West 21st Street, Suite 3B, New York, New York 10010. Printed in the United States of America.

10 9 8 7 6 5 4 3 2 1

CONTENTS

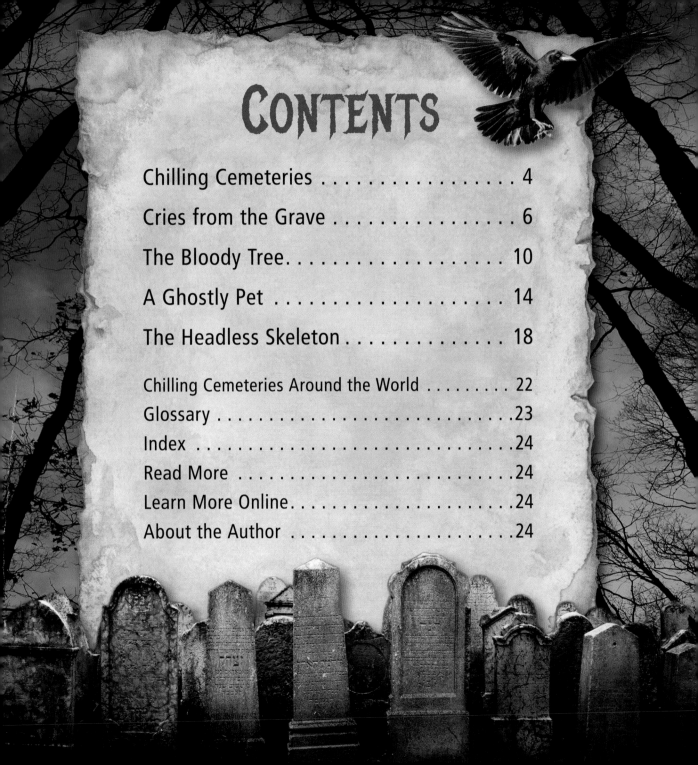

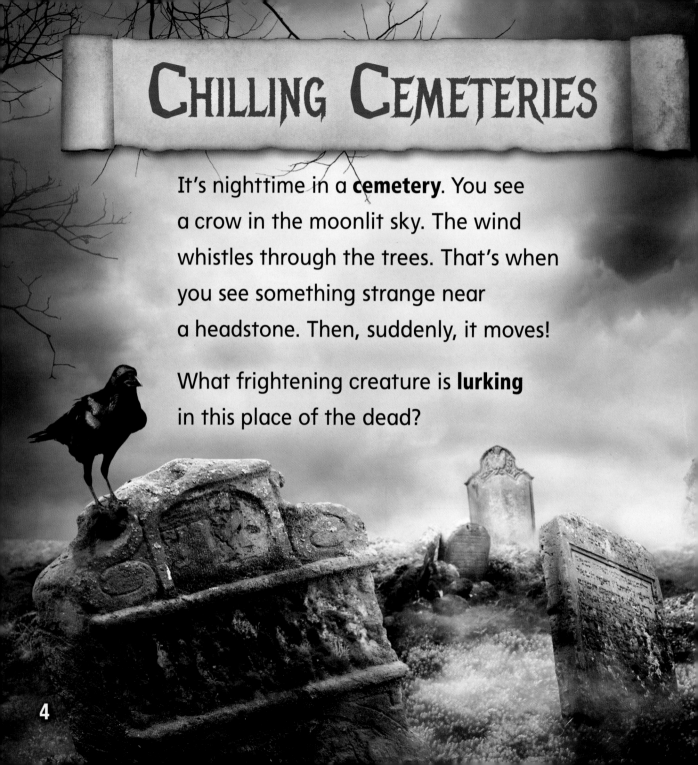

CHILLING CEMETERIES

It's nighttime in a **cemetery**. You see a crow in the moonlit sky. The wind whistles through the trees. That's when you see something strange near a headstone. Then, suddenly, it moves!

What frightening creature is **lurking** in this place of the dead?

4

Get ready to read four bone-chilling stories about haunted cemeteries. Turn the page . . . if you have the nerve!

CRIES FROM THE GRAVE

Sleepy Hollow Cemetery, New York

It was a pitch-black Halloween night in 1916. A young girl entered a cemetery on a dare.

Suddenly, she heard something odd. It was the sound of a person quietly crying.

The curious girl followed the sound.
She tiptoed around the old tombstones.
Her heart thumped wildly.

Sleepy Hollow
Cemetery

7

Finally, the girl traced the sound to a clearing. At that moment, the crying stopped. The child's eyes landed on a **bronze** statue of a seated woman.

The girl climbed into the statue's lap. Then she touched the figure's cold, metal face . . . and it was wet. Tears were streaming from the statue's eyes!

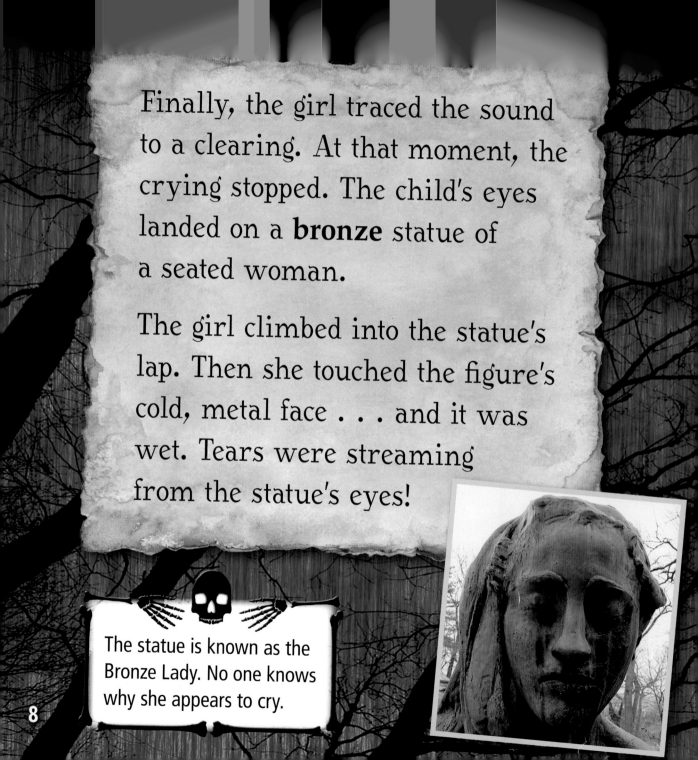

The statue is known as the Bronze Lady. No one knows why she appears to cry.

The Bronze Lady

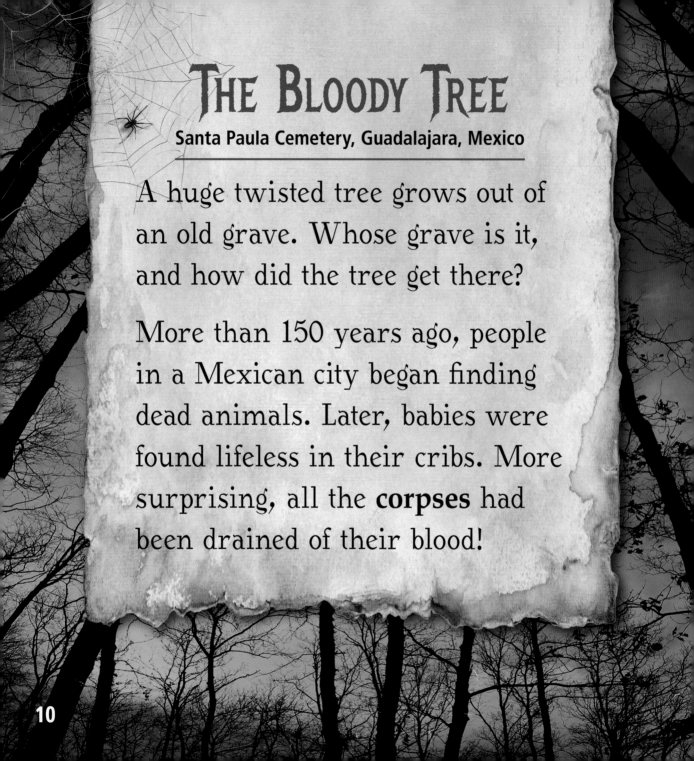

THE BLOODY TREE

Santa Paula Cemetery, Guadalajara, Mexico

A huge twisted tree grows out of an old grave. Whose grave is it, and how did the tree get there?

More than 150 years ago, people in a Mexican city began finding dead animals. Later, babies were found lifeless in their cribs. More surprising, all the **corpses** had been drained of their blood!

The tree and grave

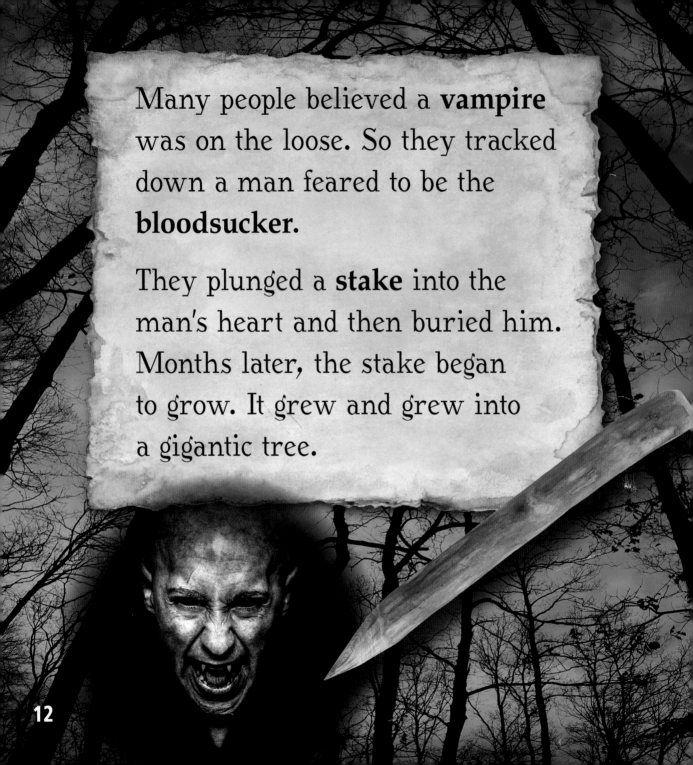

Many people believed a **vampire** was on the loose. So they tracked down a man feared to be the **bloodsucker.**

They plunged a **stake** into the man's heart and then buried him. Months later, the stake began to grow. It grew and grew into a gigantic tree.

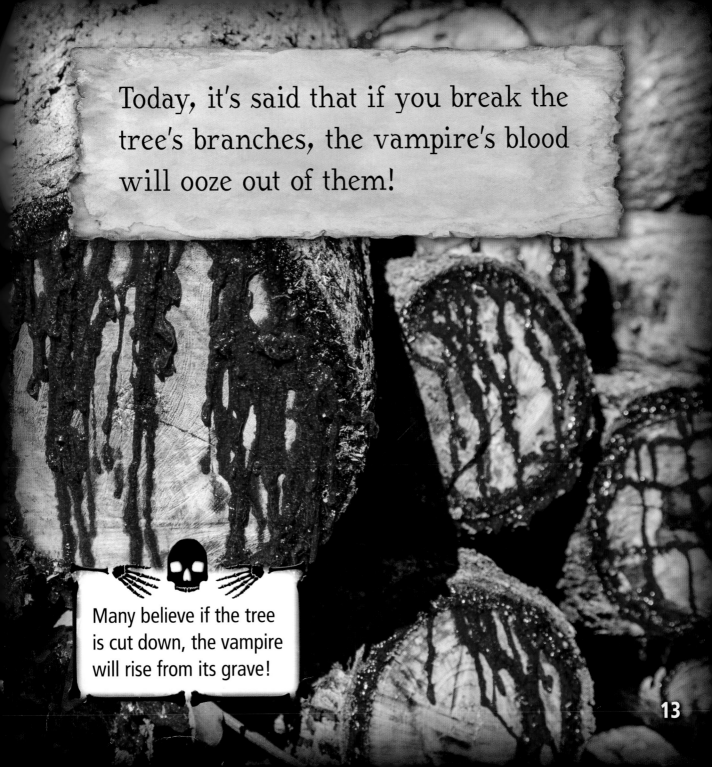

Today, it's said that if you break the tree's branches, the vampire's blood will ooze out of them!

Many believe if the tree is cut down, the vampire will rise from its grave!

A Ghostly Pet

Hollywood Cemetery, Richmond, Virginia

Can a statue come to life? Visitors to Hollywood Cemetery think so.

In 1862, a young girl died from a terrible illness. Her **grieving** family buried her body. Near her grave, they placed a statue of a dog.

When she died, the little girl was only two years old.

Since then, on cold dark nights, people have seen something unbelievable. The dog statue moves! It has been seen shifting from one spot to another.

Some say that if you get too close to the grave, the dog comes alive. It barks and runs after visitors!

The Headless Skeleton

Barnes Cemetery, London, England

Thick vines cover crumbling headstones. Mist hangs in the night air. A white, **wispy** female figure glides over one of the graves. Who is she, and what is she looking for?

Barnes Cemetery

In the 1870s, a skeleton washed up near the River Thames. Soon after, the bones were buried in Barnes Cemetery. However, one important piece was missing—the skull.

Later, it was discovered that the bones belonged to a woman who had been murdered. Could that be why a female ghost has been seen **hovering** in the cemetery?

The woman was murdered by her housekeeper. Her skull was found in 2010 near her old house.

CHILLING CEMETERIES
AROUND THE WORLD

SANTA PAULA CEMETERY
Guadalajara, Mexico

Visit a vampire's grave and a blood-filled tree!

SLEEPY HOLLOW CEMETERY
Sleepy Hollow, New York

Check out a statue that weeps!

HOLLYWOOD CEMETERY
Richmond, Virginia

Come see a child's grave and the eerie statue that protects her.

BARNES CEMETERY
London, England

Visit the final resting place of a headless skeleton.

Arctic Ocean

NORTH AMERICA

EUROPE

ASIA

Atlantic Ocean

Pacific Ocean

AFRICA

Pacific Ocean

SOUTH AMERICA

Indian Ocean

Atlantic Ocean

AUSTRALIA

Southern Ocean

ANTARCTICA

Glossary

bloodsucker (BLUHD-suhk-ur) a creature that sucks blood

bronze (BRAHNZ) a yellowish-brown metal

cemetery (SEM-uh-*terr*-ee) an area of land where dead bodies are buried

corpses (KORPS-iz) dead bodies

grieving (GREEV-ing) feeling great sadness or sorrow

hovering (HUHV-ur-ing) staying in one place in the air

lurking (LURK-ing) secretly hiding

stake (STAYK) a thick, pointed piece of wood

vampire (VAM-pire) in stories, a person who rises from the dead to feed on the blood of the living

wispy (WIS-pee) fine or feathery

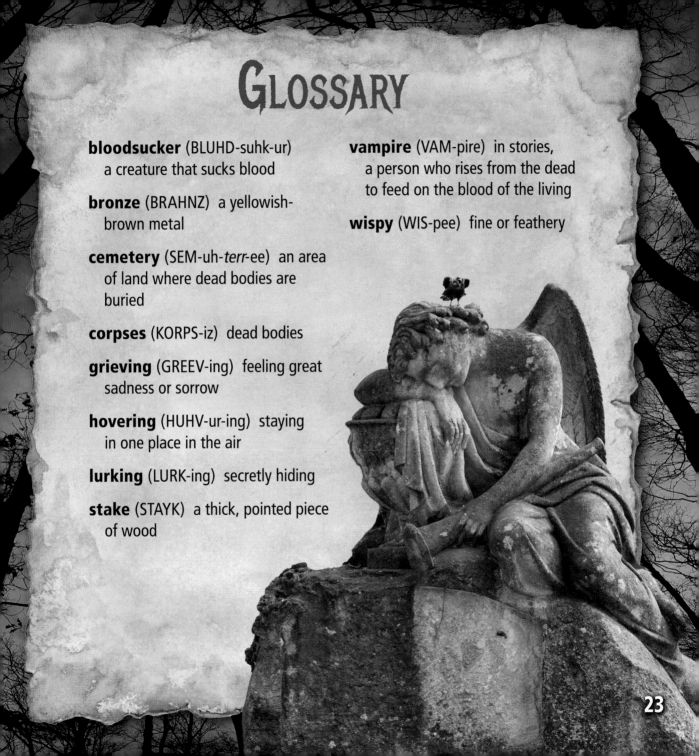

Index

Read More

Penn-Coughin, O. *They're Coming for You: Scary Stories That Scream to be Read.* New York: CreateSpace (2011).

Tietelbaum, Michael. *Night of the Gravedigger (Cold Whispers).* New York: Bearport (2016).

Learn More Online

To learn more about chilling cemeteries, visit:
www.bearportpublishing.com/Tiptoe

About the Author

Joyce Markovics is an author who lives in a 160-year-old house. Chances are a few otherworldly beings live there, too.